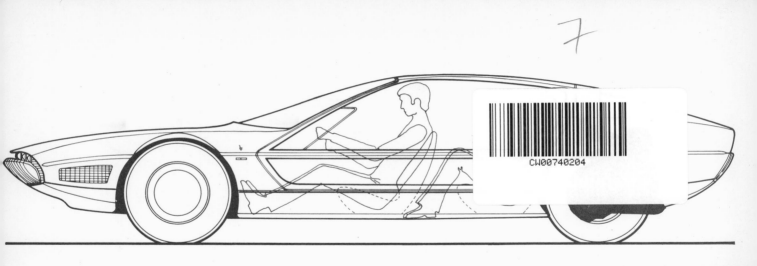

1967 - Lamborghini MARZAL

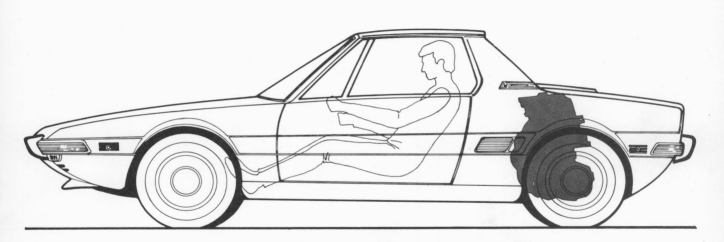

1972 - FIAT X1/9

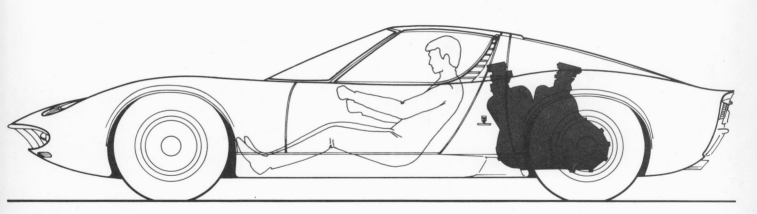

1966 - Lamborghini MIURA

ISBN 0 85429 349 3

A FOULIS Motoring Book

First published 1984

Published by:
Haynes Publishing Group
Sparkford, Yeovil, Somerset BA22 7JJ, England

Distributed in North America by:
Haynes Publication Inc.
861 Lawrence Drive, Newbury Park,
California 91320, USA

Editor: Rod Grainger
Page layout: Anne Wildey
Dust jacket picture: Lamborghini Countach, courtesy
of Chris Harvey.
Printed in England, by: J.H. Haynes & Co. Ltd

# The Automotive Art of
# BERTONE

## by Rob de la Rive Box
## & Richard Crump

Foulis

Haynes

# Author's Introduction & Acknowledgements

The world's greatest couture houses are influenced by what the Paris designers create; similarly original automobile design ideas emanate from Italy. While the car manufacturer wrestles with the problems of new model construction, he is able to call upon the resources of a number of design studios to clothe his technically new model. This book is intended to illustrate one Italian coachbuilder's art, that of the influential Carrozzeria Bertone.

The authors express their thanks to Carrozzeria Bertone, Automobile Revue, Richard Veen, Manfred Lampe and Peter Coltrin – without whose help this book would not have been possible.

# The Bertone Story

The coachbuilding company was founded, in 1912, by Giovanni Bertone who was born in 1884 at Mondovi some 60 miles from Turin. He was one of eight children in a farming family which was scraping a meagre living from the arrid land characteristic of that area of Italy. Doubtless Giovanni's father was relieved when, at the age of 12, Giovanni gained employment with a local firm building horse-drawn carriages.

With this company Giovanni learned the basic skills and techniques of construction with wood and metal, before leaving the area for Turin in 1907. At the age of 23 he gained employment with Diatto, who were then making their name with railway rolling stock, although from 1905 they had also been moving into car construction. After seven years with Diatto, Giovanni took his tools and equipment and started his own business repairing wagons and coaches in a small building with a canvas roof. Within a short time Bertone was making his own sulkies – lightweight racing buckets for the horse-racing fraternity – and his reputation for craftsmanship was increasing within the area of Turin, the birthplace of the automobile industry in Italy.

The motor car was gaining in popularity, and young Bertone, like a number of others, was both intrigued and fascinated by this new method of transportation. His longing for an association with such a growing industry led him to re-establish his contacts with Diatto, for which company he constructed the ash framework of their rolling chassis prior to delivery to a coachbuilder. At the same time he was approached by SPA to construct complete bodies on their type 9000 chassis. Bearing in mind the poor security of his small coachworks, it was arranged that each chassis be towed, by horse, from the SPA works each morning and towed back again each night until the body was completed! Only the quality of Giovanni's workmanship could have allowed such a contract with SPA.

Bertone found that it was preferable to complete several bodies to one design, the production of a limited series being more profitable to his little company and more effective for the car factories whose sales were growing quickly. In 1921 the original Bertone building was vacated and a proper factory rented in which to house the growing number of chassis that were finding their way to him and the other craftsmen he now employed. The same year he constructed, to his own design, a sporting body on a SPA 9000 chassis for Ing. Momo who then entered, and won, the Coupe des Alpes race.

Within a couple of years, Bertone's regular customers included Lancia, Ceirano, Itala, Fiat and Scat; some sending chassis, others receiving finished bodies from Bertone. For Lancia, Bertone was building bodies for the Kappa and Lambda but, in 1923, the relationship between the two companies reached a crucial stage, the outcome of which was to slow the progress Bertone was making with his own business. Basically what Vincenzo Lancia wanted was to have a metal monocoque closed body supplied in large numbers to his Turin factory, and he approached Giovanni Bertone for the business. Not unnaturally, Bertone did not like the idea and, although the scheme was to be backed up with Lancia money and technical resources, it held little interest or challenge for him. As a coachbuilder and designer, he felt that his craft would be lost in such an operation and so declined the offer from Lancia. Eventually Lancia solved his supply problem by building his own body plant, and by the late 1920s Bertone began to feel the material effects of his decision ...

By the early 1930s many of the infant Italian car builders had already gone into liquidation, or had been absorbed by the growing giant Fiat. Somehow Bertone managed to survive this difficult period by taking on individual new work and repairing damaged bodies, but it was a struggle: a struggle which he wished to share with his son. Born during the outbreak of World War I, Giovanni's son had been working in his spare time in the coachbuilding business learning the basic requirements of the trade. At 17 years of age Nuccio had passed his examinations in accountancy, and by 1932 was in his second year studying for his economics degree at Turin University. The University released him from his studies at the age of 18 and he worked alongside his father fulltime in the hope that between them they could salvage and possibly develop the Bertone coachworks.

To some extent the pair were greatly aided, if indirectly, by Fiat, which introduced the incredible Ballila in late 1933. For this tiny vehicle, Bertone designed several styles of coachwork to be built in his factory, and in 1934 Nuccio became a commercial traveller endeavouring to sell their interpretations for what was to become a popular motor car because it epitomised what the Italian car owner wanted, perfectly. The orders for the Fiat Ballilas came with a vengeance as a result of Nucio's regional sales tours, a method he used annually to increase the country's awareness of what his father's coachworks could achieve. From 1934, until the outbreak of the war, some thirty different body styles were adopted for the Ballila chassis: many upon the theme created by Bertone.

Nuccio had a personal interest in motor racing which, although shared cautiously by his father, was not welcomed by his mother. During his six years travelling throughout Italy and Sicily with the portfolio of coachwork designs, Nuccio managed to visit many race meetings where he made valuable contacts with many of the Italian industry's important and influential owners and suppliers. By 1940 Nuccio's life was totally immersed in the motor car, and father and son managed to avert the bankruptcy which had threatened their little company at the crossroads with Lancia in 1923. During the war years, military work took precedence and, although occupied to the full, times for the Bertone factory were hard and austere. From 1946 with the Italian car industry in disarray, it being impossible to obtain any chassis upon which to build bodies, Nuccio drifted back to his motor racing interests.

Between 1946 and the early 1950s he competed in mountain racing, hillclimbing and speed events with Fiat 500 and 750 models, graduating eventually to circuit racing in events such as the Targa Florio and Mille Miglia in OSCA, Stanguellini, Maserati and Ferrari. There were no major accidents during his leisurely life as an amateur racing driver, and not only did the sport re-establish prewar contacts with many important people but it also allowed Nuccio to gain valuable insights to the competitive aspects of the car industry. However this new lifestyle for the young Nuccio was in reality hiding the fact that his father's company was again in a bad financial state. Coupled to the postwar difficulties of rebuilding of his own business, the Italian motor industry was struggling to find its feet and this greatly affected Giovanni Bertone's volume of work. Additionally there was galloping postwar inflation to cope with.

In 1950 Nuccio and his father had purchased two MG chassis and had the original MG bodies removed; they then designed and built their own coupe and cabriolet bodies on these already rather vintage chassis. With literally their last available lire, Carrozzeria Bertone purchased an exhibition stand in an inexpensive corner of the auditorium where the Turin automobile show of 1952 was to take place. Their hope was to attract, through those two Bertone MGs, at least one motor manufacturer who would see the style and quality of their workmanship and place some work orders with the company. The events which transpired as a result of this show were to be the family's life-saver and even three decades later can be seen as being most important in the history of Bertone.

Browsing through the Turin show admiring the work of Vignale, Ghia, Boano and Zagato was Stanley Harold Arnolt II, a 45-year-old wealthy Chicago businessman and self-confessed MG enthusiast. Obviously Arnolt had never before seen an Italian-bodied MG, but Bertone's cabriolet and coupe on the MGTD chassis worked wonders for his pulse rate and enlivened his financial thoughts. After the shortest of interviews, Arnolt and Nuccio Bertone went to the coachworks to discuss a regular supply of MGs to Chicago, where Arnolt was based as the largest BMC distributor for the American midwest. Agreement was reached between the two companies for 200 Bertone-bodied MGs to be shipped to S. H. Arnolt Inc. for exclusive distribution in the USA and to be known as 'Arnolt-MG'. Finance was not a problem for Arnolt who arranged both payment for, and shipment of, chassis from the MG factory at Abingdon-on-Thames to the Port of Genoa and then by road and rail to Turin. Once each body had been completed by Bertone, the finished car was returned to Genoa and shipped to Arnolt in Illinois. The Arnolt-MG coupe sold for 3000 dollars in Chicago and was the cheapest Italian-bodied sports car available in that market; the obvious advantage of the model being that any MG dealership throughout America could service the car.

By the Summer of 1953, 200 Arnolt-MGs had been completed by Bertone, and Arnolt was established as Carrozzeria Bertone's sole agent in the USA. These two businessmen, one craftsman, one entrepreneur, created the Arnolt-Bristol in 1953: another Italian design for the solid 404 Bristol chassis. The new model was shown for the first time at the London Motor Show in November 1953 and eventually in total 130 Arnolt-Bristols were finished: three coupes and the others Bolides, race cars used by the Arnolt-Bristol racing team, and dropheads.

Although the relationship with Arnolt did little to stimulate Bertone's profit, it certainly did enable the company to work on other projects which came their way as a direct result of building the MGs. Factory personnel were no longer uncertain about their future and the carrozzeria could be seen by others to be working at full capacity: a psychological advantage. The end of the bad postwar phase was in sight by the end of 1952, a year in which Bertone had exhibited his highly original Abarth coupe creation at the Paris Salon. Although expressly designed for the show in Paris, the model was previewed by the management of Packard who immediately purchased the Bertone Abarth before the Salon opened its doors. It was without doubt one of the most radical designs of the year, but was a hint of what one could expect from Bertone in the future ... In 1953 a tentative approach from Alfa Romeo introduced Bertone to the problems of aerodynamics with special reference to streamlining in the pursuit of high performance. Known for their interest in racing and quick road cars, the Alfa Romeo factory were looking for a coachbuilder who could design and construct a body for their intended Disco Volante, and Carrozzeria Bertone were virtually on their doorstep. Negotiations between the two companies took some while before an agreement was reached for Bertone to build on the 1900SS chassis – his own interpretation of a two-seater coupe capable of giving maximum performance with high fuel economy. What emerged in 1953 was the Berlina Aerodinamica Tecnica designed by Franco Scaglione, built by Bertone and correctly hailed as one of the most outrageous designs ever produced. This Alfa Romeo was labelled BAT-5, since the previous four designs were abandoned with design failures in one area or another. The BAT-5 car was driven on several occasions at speeds in excess of 120mph which encouraged the Alfa Romeo management to continue their streamlining programme with Bertone. Number six of the BAT series did not materialise; BAT-7 emerged as an even wilder shape and delivered a slightly higher speed with a further small improvement in economy. Alfa Romeo nodded approvingly at Bertone to continue the theme. However the next BAT design was to hold greater appeal as a practical GT car, which Alfa Romeo could market to the public. In 1954 the result of this brief was the BAT-9.

Through the BAT-series of the early fifties, Bertone and his staff gained an enormous amount of publicity – and not solely in his home market. Although the Bertone company BAT designs were disliked by many, his creativity was encouraged by certain automotive journalists as being a major styling breakthrough in the postwar gloom of the automotive industry. Through this collaboration with Alfa Romeo emerged the famous Giulietta Sprint on the 1300 chassis, of which over 40,000 examples would be sold during the period 1954-1967. During these years the Bertone coachworks became established and, in 1959, moved to Grugliasco near Turin to occupy a substantial new factory large enough for future expansion in all areas of their work.

Not unnaturally Bertone's successes brought forth from other manufacturers briefs for design and construction on a wide variety of chassis. Almost all automobile constructors at one time or another turned towards Bertone to sculpt creations that could achieve volume sales for their cars. Not all his work was with the volume car manufacturers; in 1956 Abarth wanted a speed record car to be constructed by Bertone based on the ubiquitous 750 Fiat. Bertone's slippery design resulted in new International speed records for Abarth, the 395kg special breaking eleven records in the 500-750 International Class H division.

1957 saw the arrival of the Giulietta SS coupe for Alfa Romeo in which could be clearly seen the BAT influence. This was a more sporting version of the 2-plus-2 Sprint and gained favour with many customers looking for a quick, good-looking motor car.

Through a Bertone design exercise on a private customer's 250GT Ferrari in early 1960, Nuccio Bertone gained from Enzo Ferrari the commission for the one-litre Ferrarina design. This small fastback coupe materialised in 1961 and the project was sold by Ferrari to the ASA company. Financially the ASA group was insecure and, after a few examples were finished, the group went into receivership. A 1600 version on an Innocenti chassis was developed by Ferrari and Bertone, but this too floundered.

During the early 1960s a new designer's name emerged under the Bertone umbrella, that of Giorgio Giugiaro. He assisted with a one-off 250GT Ferrari in 1962, and although his design was considerably more pleasing than the production 250GT, Ferrari maintained his close working relationship with Pinin Farina.

Each year Bertone endeavoured to announce a major new design for a car manufacturer, usually displayed on its own at one of the many European salons. In 1963 it was the Testudo on a Corvair Monza chassis and in 1964 came the fabulous Canguro constructed in aluminium on the Alfa Romeo competition TZ.2 chassis. Unfortunately the GTZ was performing admirably for the manufacturer at the time, so the Italian 'Kangaroo' was not adopted for production and remained a dream car. In 1965 the Bertone team restyled the Mustang for Ford in the USA, and the following year exhibited the Miura for Lamborghini. The latter came from the pen of Marcello Gandini who had replaced Giugiaro as chief designer. It is history that Ferruccio Lamborghini adopted this Bertone creation which, together with the Miura S and SV models, put the ex-tractor manufacturer on the automotive map. Without doubt the Miura gained world-wide acceptance as a supercar, and from its initial showing in 1966 through the following six years of its life it remained a classic. It was the epitome of the aggressive, large capacity sports racer that appealed to so many, and only after production had ceased did Ferruccio Lamborghini realise that he could have manufactured the model for another ten years since demand continually outstripped supply. Still playing with the charging black bull, in 1967 came the Marzal from Bertone which effectively was the prototype of the Espada, a large four-seater touring GT.

For 1968 the Bertone creation was the Carabo, built on one of the tipo 33 competition Alfa Romeo chassis. Named after the green and black carabus beetle, the dream car was shown at Paris in early 1968. With its forward hinging doors and totally committed wedge shape this creation did indeed look like a beetle, but the decision that it would remain a prototype only came as no surpirse. The Carabo was chosen some four years after its initial showing as being a significant design which would represent the automobile world at an exhibition organised by the Museum of the Twentieth Century in Vienna. Upon reflection it can be seen that both the Lamborghini Urraco of 1970, and the prototype Stratos for Lancia, were directly descended from the Carabo. These wedge-shaped two-seater coupes were popular and aerodynamically successful. In 1973 Bertone gave Ferrari the 308 GT4, an assignment he got following the Fiat takeover of Ferrari in 1969.

During the ten year period just described not all Bertone designs were show cars or prototypes, for Nuccio Bertone was an excellent organiser and businessman. In 1964 for Fiat, Bertone had built the 850 sports coupe from which came the highly successful Fiat 850 spider. How successful this small convertible was can be illustrated by looking at the sales figures during its first production year of 1965 when the total was 8500. After this production increased at the rate of over 30% per year until 1970 during which year over 31,000 units were made! The American market consumed 90% of the Fiat Bertone spiders of which a total of 140,000 were built, and for some time it was the top selling Italian car on the U.S. market.

By 1973 the Fiat X1/9 had arrived with its wedge shape and mid-engine, and this served Fiat well as a replacement for the 850 spider, attaining high sales in the USA.

The 1970s saw truly astonishing designs emerge from Bertone – the Miura's successor, the Countach for Lamborghini; the highly desirable Stratos for Lancia; the elegant Khamsin for Maserati (now under de Tomaso control) and the prototype Trapeze based on the R080 for NSU. In 1976 for Alfa Romeo came the Navajo, built on a lengthened tipo 33 chassis, and some day a car which could emerge as a production Alfa.

Nuccio Bertone pictured in his office during 1983.

In the 1980s the first Bertone designs for the staid Swedish manufacturer Volvo were completed. A new star was created for Lamborghini, the Athon, which could be produced in limited numbers by the Sant'Agata company now under French control. Also Carrozzeria Bertone played with the fashionable off-road vehicle market for Fiat and Simca, and returned to soft-top design for Fiat with the Strada/Ritmo Cabrio. At the same time the incredible MX-81 was created for Mazda in early 1982.

In his late fifties, Nuccio Bertone continues to run his company with enormous vigour. His father, Giovanni, died in 1972 at the age of 88 but not before he had seen the company pull itself from the near disasters of the pre and postwar times into being a major industrial company with a secure reputation and future. The scope of Bertone and his designers is seemingly endless: he has the ability to create wonderful cars by moulding together the improbable and the possible and making dreams come true. Carrozzeria Bertone are masters of their art, a fact which they regularly illustrate with skill, flair and vision.

# The Pre-war Period

Ash framework from Bertone craftsmen on a 1921 10.4hp **Ceirano** chassis. This would have been completed in the style of a four-seater tourer which the Ceirano factory of Turin were successfully selling in the period 1920-1930.

For **Autocostruzioni Diatto** of Turin, Bertone built a comfortable four-seater saloon body on this 1924 Tipo 20.

There is an area of doubt concerning the coachbuilder of this 1919 **Fiat** 501. Those at Bertone appear to think it was one of the firm's creations not very accurately christened 'Balloon'. The 501 was really the first model to be mass-produced by the Fiat company which today is one of the world's automobile giants.

The front wings remain horizontal while the rears have distinctly dropped. This is a 1919 **Fiat** 505 landaulet.

‹ Bertone's treatment of a 1924 **Fiat** 505 which one imagines, from its sporting image, had the 3.4-litre six-cylinder engine.

‹ A charming if somewhat per-pendicular **Fiat** 509 landaulet taxi from Bertone. One can imagine being swiftly transported through the Turin streets by an enthusiastic taxi-driver anxious for his lire.

**Fiat** also commissioned Bertone for ›
their brief competition career. This is one of the 1923 501S cars.

Proof that the **Fiat** Corsa 501 was a two-seater. The car was attractive and 'skimpy' in design, and probably not as quick as its appearance would suggest.
⌄

In 1932 **Fiat** introduced their advanced small car the Balilla. Bertone created this four-door style much helped by the use of two-tone paintwork.

The same **Fiat** chassis but produced as a convertible by Bertone. One can imagine the soft top Balilla suited many Italians.

An example of pre-war sales material from Bertone showing his convertible on the 508 C chassis introduced by **Fiat** in 1938.

The six-cylinder **Fiat** 527 was produced from 1936 to 1940 in large numbers. There were many variations, one being this well-proportioned aero-dynamic saloon.

Another version of the **Fiat** 527, this time with four doors and recessed headlamps.

The sporting approach. This **Fiat** 1500-based design was probably too 'spangled' for many customers.

A four-seater convertible on the 1500 >
**Fiat** – more lustre and three hinges for
each door.

Bertone created this 'panoramica' on a
1934 **Fiat** 518 Ardita 2000 chassis. It
looks immensely comfortable.
∨

Doubtless the Italian Al Capones would have purchased this Bertone designed **Fiat** Ardita.

A truly incredible line, again **Fiat** Ardita-based. The headlamp cowls return as far as the rear wings; the front bumper profile is repeated in radiator and bonnet.

It might seem that Bertone was inundated with the large **Fiats.** On this 2800 of 1938/9 he turned the door handles vertical, perhaps as a gesture of boredom?

The beginnings of a long relationship with the respected **Lancia** factory. This is a 1922 Trikappa town carriage from Bertone.

Another elegant **Lancia** Trikappa; the speaking tube for chauffeur is clearly visible.

*Berlina Artena ì 6 porti*

< 1929 **Lancia** Lambda, presumably 9th series chassis, which made excellent taxis for the Italian family man.

< In 1929 Bertone constructed this coupe de ville body on a **Lancia** Artena chassis. A good car for fine weather.

A six passenger, four door **Lancia** ∧ Artena. The side windows were quite narrow in comparison with the overall height thus creating a 'stand up and enter' limousine.

Sporting wire wheels and twin spares, ⟩ the likeable style of Bertone's 1934 **Lancia** Augusta.

For the front cover of a sales brochure, Bertone chose his design for a **Lancia** Aprilia. The doors are rear opening with an artistic curvature in door and wing, subtly repeated in the bonnet.

What Bertone did for Fiat he could almost do for the **Lancia** Aprilia!

Highly decorative wheel trims and plenty of chrome: another **Lancia** Aprilia.

1938 **Lancia** Aprilia four-seater from Bertone somehow did not fall easily on the eye. The rear appears to be leaning forward while the frontal aspect appears short.

Unlike many coachbuilders of the early 1920s Bertone resisted the urge to place the sidelights on top of the wings. The 30/40hp **S.P.A.** with its V-radiator was an impressive looking sports tourer. (E1)

The lovely 1921 **S.P.A.** model 9000 with a Bertone torpedo style body. The rear passengers were obliged to climb up into their seats, since no rear doors were fitted. (D1)

# The Forties & Fifties

^
For **Abarth** in 1952. Bertone designed this two seater coupe. Not pretty, but style it certainly had.

< From three-quarter rear of the **Abarth** it would seem Bertone had gone heavily into curves. The complex shape of the rear window is highlighted with a spar.

The frontal aspect of the same **Abarth** > was exciting, if somewhat daunting. A certain pontoon effect gives a feeling for what the designer was trying to achieve.

This aerodynamic shell was created for **Abarth** to cheat the wind on the Monza track in 1956. Driven in relay by six automobile journalists, the Abarth collected ten new speed records.

The Bertone-designed **Abarth** record car on the Monza banking in 1956.

A rarely seen view of the **Abarth** record car. No Kamm principle, but the period feathering of the tail undoubtedly was effective.

Pictured in April 1956, the type 215/A **Abarth** from Bertone. The wheel trims appear strangely out of style with the three-eared spinners, but the overall appearance is pleasing.

Bertone retained his frontal design from 1952 for this pretty 1000 **Abarth** sport.

Pictured at the Turin show in 1958, the overall design was well proportioned and compact.

The first postwar Bertone design was executed on this 1945 **Alfa Romeo** 6C-2500 chassis. Although a clean line and unobtrusive grille treatment was achieved the car somehow looked very sad.

The spider version of the 1945 **Alfa Romeo** 2500. Surprisingly Bertone created nothing new for the wheel arches which resulted in this particular model appearing too high from the ground.

A technical design exercise on behalf of **Alfa Romeo** resulted in the **B.A.T.** The finished Bertone creation is seen at Turin in 1953.

The **B.A.T.** was actually built on an **Alfa Romeo** 1900S chassis. Four designs from Bertone were rejected before this version was commissioned.

Known as **B.A.T.** 5 it can be imagined what criticism Bertone and **Alfa Romeo** suffered as a result of this show stopper.

With improved aerodynamics this is the **Alfa Romeo B.A.T.** 7 constructed in 1954. There never was a B.A.T.6

The rear style of the **Alfa Romeo B.A.T.** 8 was slightly altered and the Alfa Romeo badge incorporated below the central spine.

Bertone removed the rear wheel spats; incorporated plexiglass headlamp covers and the correct **Alfa Romeo** grille for **B.A.T.** 9.

The overall design was cleaner and according to the staff at Bertone more efficient: The **Alfa Romeo B.A.T.** 9 in 1955.

Note how the vertical door lines blend with the forward slanting window pillars. It was sad that **Alfa Romeo** did not continue the **B.A.T.** theme, for who knows where Bertone would have gone with the styling?

Only three **B.A.T. Alfa Romeos** were built and they were all sold in the U.S.A. One is seen here at Palm Springs in 1955.

The same car obviously ready for a straight-line sprint. The 'bandages' somehow seem unnecessary.

An important car for Bertone, the **Alfa Romeo** Giulietta Sprint of 1954.

The style of the **Alfa Romeo** was very pleasing: clean design with practical proportions.

By the time Bertone had finished with the Giulietta 'egg crate' **Alfa Romeo** had built over 40,000 examples in 13 years' production life.

A one-off 1955 Giulietta which **Alfa Romeo** called a spider and Bertone a cabriolet.

Almost ready for a run in the Mille Miglia! The Sportiva was created by Bertone on a four-cylinder two-litre **Alfa Romeo** chassis in 1955.

The **Alfa Romeo** Sportiva looked superb, with its rear end design reminiscent of the **B.A.T.** The Bertone style was certainly apparent with this spider.

The 1956 coupe version of the **Alfa Romeo** Sportiva was a delicious design. It looked as though it could travel fast forever.

From the rear the only criticism may have been the size of the licence plate. Only two **Alfa Romeo** Sportiva coupes were constructed.

Bertone called this convertible 'Perla' (pearl) built on a 1955 **Alfa Romeo** 1900 chassis.

Seen on the **Alfa Romeo** stand at the Turin show in October 1957, was this Bertone Sprint Special.

The first 153 **Alfa Romeo** Giulietta SSs had aluminium bodies; after 1959 the coachwork was in steel. Shown here is a 1960 model.

Certainly the SSs built after 1959 were not as pretty as the earlier examples. Probably because it had become a semi-production unit for **Alfa Romeo** and lost some of its original one-off style.

With the hardtop removed, and viewed from this angle the same car was neither attractive nor likeable.

On a 2000 **Alfa Romeo** chassis Bertone designed the 'Sole e Luce' in 1959. It retained some of the styling characteristics of his 'Perla'.

The **Alfa Romeo** Sprint 2000 coupe exhibited at the Turin show in 1960. It seemed that Bertone had still not made a decision on whether rear wheel arches should be highlighted, or blended with the rest of the car

From the rear the design was clean and effective. This four-cylinder **Alfa Romeo** was a popular model, although later replaced by the six-cylinder 2600 engine.

For **Arnolt,** Bertone designed and built ⟩
this coupe, or berlina, on the 1952
MG TD chassis.

⌃
Photographed in the U.S.A. in 1952,
the **Arnolt** MG coupe certainly had a
distinctive line. The Bertone emblem
can be seen low down near the door
opening.

Naturally the soft top or convertible ⟩
version of the **Arnolt** MG warranted
wire wheels to endorse the sporting
image.

However, on this convertible, no wire wheels! The frontal treatment by Bertone was if anything a little austere, but the model greatly appealed to the American market of the time.

With the **Arnolt** seen from this angle the image of an E-type Jaguar creeps through. The rear wheel arches appear large but the overall design is pleasing.

For **Arnolt** the Aston Martin was also
clothed by Bertone. The blend of vertical bumpers into the grille was neat
and calm.

On a later DB2/4 Aston Martin chassis, the grille treatment of the **Arnolt** has changed completely and the air scoop has disappeared. The horse-rider looks quite unhappy about the whole affair!

On the Bristol 404 chassis Bertone created this lovely sports body for **Arnolt** in 1955. The two very long straps were, one feels, just a gimmick.

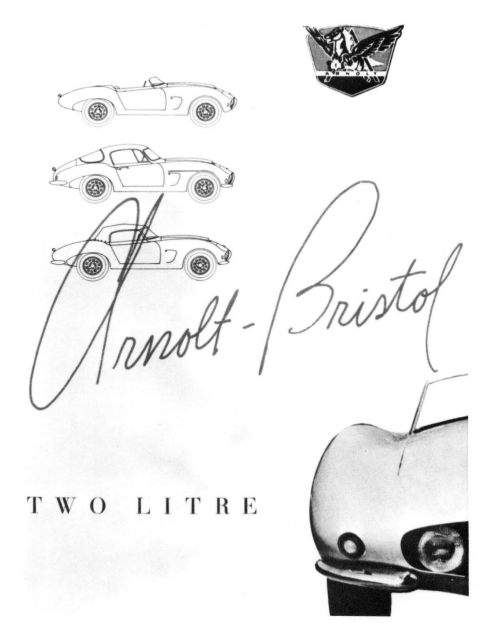

*Arnolt-Bristol*

TWO LITRE

From **Arnolt's** sales brochure showing ⟩
the three Bertone creations for the
Bristol chassis. The coupe, the deluxe
and the 'Bolide'.

< The **Arnolt** Bristol coupe of 1953. Certainly a handsome car which sold well in America.

< Designed for competition use in the U.S.A. this particular **Arnolt** Bristol model was popular. The front wheel arches have returned to normal style and the headlamps on top of the bonnet have disappeared.

< Seen at the Paris Salon in October 1956, the open version of Bertone's design for **Arnolt** has matured, and the windscreen had gained a central pillar.

The **Arnolt** Bristol Mk II coupe fitted with Boranni spinners. One can understand Bertone's excitement at creating this car: the rear is smooth and uncluttered, and the boot lid contours interesting.

Audience response to the **Arnolt** Bristol was better than this picture would indicate! The grille appears almost as an afterthought but is saved by the mounting of twin foglamps.

On the **Aston Martin** DB2/4 chassis Bertone designed this convertible in 1953.

From the front the **Aston Martin** has a hard appearance; the bonnet has an unmistakable Bertone look.

Neat hood stowage of the **Aston Martin**: altogether a clean shape without fancy fins and lights.

In 1957 the Bertone created **Aston Martin** DB III was not one of his better designs. Again the wheel arches suffered from indecision.

From this angle the Bertone **Aston Martin** looks uninteresting and not very sporting. A similar design was to adorn a Maserati chassis in 1959.

Reputedly built for Arnolt in 1953, this Mk VII **Bentley** had a high waist line with reduced roof height. One gets the impression that Bertone lacked courage with the product.

In 1952 a two-door **Borgward** coupe received the Bertone treatment.

For the American car manufacturer **Dodge,** this two-door coupe was shown at Turin in 1954 by Bertone.

From the front the **Dodge** 'Zeder' >
design may have inspired Facel Vega
some six years later.

For **Ferrari** on the 1950 type 166 Inter >
chassis, this rather conservative
cabriolet.

Bertone's design for this **Ferrari** was >
hardly innovative: although the plastic
gearlever knob was a slight adventure
at the time.

Continuing his relationship with **Fiat**, Bertone offered this convertible on the 1100cc chassis in 1945.

Very stylised **Fiat** 1100 TV from Bertone. Again this coachbuilder's design for the front, incorporating grille, lights and bumper, was interesting.

The eyebrows over the wheel arches of this **Fiat** were also used by Pinin Farina for his 1947 Maserati. The style is certainly attractive. This model remained a prototype.

In 1948 on the same **Fiat** chassis, Bertone produced the four-seater convertible. Does it have the general appearance of a Morris Minor?

Interior of the same Bertone **Fiat**. One usually associates such design with American automobiles ...

Bertone retained two doors for this six-seater **Fiat** 1500 E in 1949 which created a rather sombre effect.

Also in 1951, Bertone produced his **Fiat** 'Golden Arrow'. The three side 'portholes' did not upset the design, but the silly air scoops were trivial.

The **Fiat** 'Western Arrow' coupe of 1951 was more interesting, and gave a real impression of speed.

The 1400 **Fiat** of 1951 was clothed by Bertone in coupe ...

... and convertible form.

Being a car enthusiast himself, Nuccio Bertone created this **Fiat**-based spider Corsa for his own use ...

... the V8-engined machine was the epitome of an Italian sports racer of the period.

For **Healey,** this cabriolet was over-bodied and unexciting.

The rising line of the boot and large wing area were later dropped on the production **Lancia** Aurelia.

Completed in 1948, the grille of the **Healey** shows a strong American influence, and the car has wide doors and a long overhang beyond the rear wheels.

Certainly not as pleasing as the production **Lancia** Aurelia coupe was this Bertone design on the 1952 chassis.

A six-seater **Lancia** B15 Aurelia berlina of 1953.

A strange looking small car for **NSU** was the Prinz introduced by Bertone in September 1958.

In total some 20,000 of these **NSU** cars were built; almost 3,000 in Italy from 1958 to 1962, the remainder in Germany until 1967.

For **Maserati** on their successful 3500 GT chassis, Bertone created this one-off two-door design in 1959.

**Maserati** remained with Touring of Milan for their coupe bodies on the 3.5-litre chassis, but the Bertone design was, nevertheless, not without a certain elegance.

With no hint of the company's competition pedigree, the 1959 **OSCA** coupe from Bertone. The car was actually more Fiat than individual OSCA.

Another version with different air intake and no sign of the **OSCA** identification. This is the 1960 coupe version.

A gorgeous looking Bertone spider on the 1952 **Siata** 2000 CS chassis. This is serial number 0025, powered by a V8 Chrysler engine.

The Gran Sport two seat **Siata** 208S of ⟩ 1953 with the Fiat V8 engine.

Delightful contours and symmetrical ⟩ design for the **Siata** roof.

⟨ The front treatment shows some similarity to the Arnolt-Bristol, but Bertone's grille design is more bearable on the **Siata**

For **Simca** in 1959, the 'Lido' from Bertone.

The **Simca** 1000 coupe was a dashing small car which became very popular in France.

The Bertone-built bodies for **Simca** 1000 coupes being economically transported by rail for assembly in France.

This attractive 1953 **Stanguellini** 1100 coupe shows Bertone's clean line with its distinctive rear wheel arches and slightly raised fins.

< The front of the **Stanguellini** also highlights his continuing theme of endeavouring to blend grille, bumper, bonnet and lights.

This outrageous creation for **Stanguellini** came from Bertone in 1957; it was on the Fiat 1200 chassis.

This **Stanguellini** was known as the 'Spider America': its similarity to the 1954/5 Chevrolet Corvette cannot be missed.

Compare Bertone's design for the 1953 **Stanguellini** with the same overhead view of the Siata.

# The Sixties

In reality designed for **Abarth,** the 1000 Fiat Abarth O.T.R. The ribbed air outlets used extensively by Bertone at the rear of this small raceabout were by now fashionable.

For **Alfa Romeo,** in 1961, the 2600HS  (High Speed). A lovely design but still the rear wing treatment was high-lighted to no great effect.

In 1962 a convertible 2000 Spring **Alfa Romeo** to special order.

The least expensive version of the 2600 series **Alfa Romeo** was this Bertone design for their four door six-seater saloon.

Bertone designed and built the bodies for the 1750/2000 series **Alfa Romeos.**

And the most expensive in the same **Alfa Romeo** series was this 1962 coupe. The spider versions were constructed by Touring of Milan.

Finished illustration showing proposed >
interior of the **Alfa Romeo** Montreal.

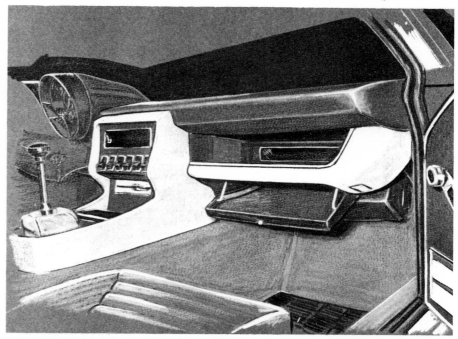

< Shown in 1967 the delicious Montreal
for **Alfa Romeo.** This was the
prototype design from Bertone which
underwent few alterations before limited production.

∨

The production model **Alfa Romeo Montreal** on show at Geneva in early 1971. The waist line has risen; rear arches are squared off and side air intakes reduced in number.

The Canguro from Bertone; a truly
fabulous design. Built in 1964 on the
Giulia 1600 **Alfa Romeo** chassis, the
Canguro design was totally functional.

The interior of the Alfa Romeo-based Canguro was slightly more comfortable than a competition car. The driver used the rev counter while the passenger was unnerved by a speedometer!

The complicated tubular chassis from **Alfa Romeo** which carried Bertone's Canguro design...

...And what happened to the chassis when the Canguro was involved in an accident.

The layout for Bertone's 1968 **Alfa Romeo**, the Carabo. >

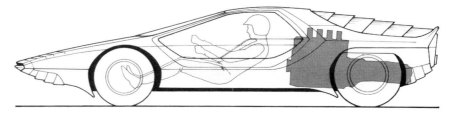

1968 - Alfa Romeo CARABO

The tipo 33 sports racing Alfa Romeo > inspired the Carabo which Bertone displayed at the 1968 Paris Salon.

What can one say? The Carabo con- > trols.

The **A.S.A.** 1000 was first shown in 1961 at the Turin show. The four-cylinder one-litre engine produced 91bhp and the car would exceed 110mph, mainly attributable to Bertone's aerodynamic design.

Christened 'Jet' this design was on an **Aston Martin** DB4GT chassis. Shown by Bertone at the 1961 Geneva motor show.

The style changed little over the model's long life, and in 1964 looked much the same as in 1961. The A.S.A. was sold in limited numbers owing mainly to its high price.

The tail of Bertone's 'Jet' had the look of a Lusso Ferrari.

A spider **A.S.A.** 1000 shown at Geneva in 1964, also by Bertone.

A Bertone dreamcar for the A112 **Autobianchi** chassis.

Interior of the **Autobianchi** 'Runabout' >
was simple and colourful.

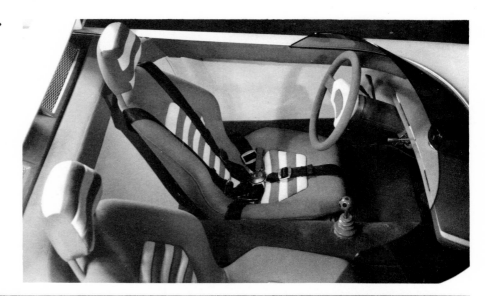

In reality. Shown in 1969 the 'Runabout' was capable of carrying two
people in an individual fashion, and
with some economy.
∨

Designed for **Bizzarini** in 1962/3 was this brutal Iso Grifo used for racing.

The powerful Iso Grifo coupe with **Bizzarini** chassis and Bertone body.

To a similar specification, came the spider version of Iso's Chevrolet-powered special.

A slightly different racing version of the **Bizzarini** with riveted aluminium front section.

<A redesign for the **BMW** 3200SC coupe by Bertone was shown at the 1963 Frankfurt motor show.

A finished design proposal from Bertone in 1969 for **BMW's** 2002TI.
∨

A prototype from Bertone on the 2800 > **BMW** chassis, called 'Spicup'. The 'Spicup' was seen at Geneva in 1969. It never went into production, but this prototype was eventually sold in Germany.

In practice the result was the **BMW** 2200 'Garmisch' in 1970. The rear glass was covered with a honeycomb section design not totally in keeping with the BMW image ...

A Bertone-bodied 250 S.W.B. **Ferrari** completed, in 1960, on chassis number 1739GT.

The **Ferrari** emblem placed on the grille was relatively small, yet strangely the bonnet badge was larger than usual. The headlamp stoneguards were a novel feature, rarely seen on postwar cars.

The BMW's interior was styled for the executive. Located in front of the passenger was a drawer unit which, when unlocked, revealed a large mirror: presumably for the secretary!

A delicious **Ferrari** 250GT! Designed by Giorgio Giugiaro while working at Bertone, and exhibited at Geneva in 1962.

The nose had a similarity with the **Ferrari** GP cars of the same period. This steel-bodied S.W.B. 250 was Nuccio Bertone's personal car; chassis number was 3269.

The egg-crate construction at Bertone in late 1962 for the proposed 'Testudo'. Mounted on the **Chevrolet** Corvair running gear, although General Motors were not involved, the car remained a prototype.

The pretty Bertone 850 **Fiat** spider introduced in 1965. Few would have expected this to become one of the most popular Italian cars for the American market. In 1968 some 120 cars a day were leaving the Fiat plant, of those 90% went to U.S.A.

The same 850 **Fiat** spider but with covered headlamps and optional hard-top.

A star-spangled **Fiat** 128 four-seater coupe at the Turin show in 1969.

Bertone gave thought to the housewife with this design for a built-in supermarket trolley. One can imagine the chaos this caused!

Voted 'Best of Show' at Geneva in 1967 was the **Fiat** 'Dino' designed by Bertone.

The **Fiat** 125 'Executive' by Bertone was an unusual design, its very angular body featuring sharp unflattering edges.

The **Fiat** was fitted with the two-litre V6 Dino engine developed by Ferrari. A clever design by Bertone gave this performance car adequate room for four passengers.

The Mustang was exhibited at the 1965 New York show. The headlamps were actually hidden behind the grille, appearing only in the dark.

This design on the **Gordon Keeble** appeared at Geneva in 1960. Owing to production difficulties with the maker the model was not available until 1964. The bodies were built in England, and only on sale until 1967.

A genuine 2-plus-2-seater **Ford** Mustang. Not unlike the Dino engined Fiat, but the rear screen received a gentler approach from Bertone.

The **Iso Rivolta** A/3 Lusso Grifo. A large and powerful motor car with 'eye' shades and 'saucer' style bonnet. The rear style had Bertone's mark as did the horizontal slatted air scoops. Is the tail a Marcos?

The spider version of the **Iso** as seen at Geneva in 1964.

And finally the 'Targa' version of the ▷
**Iso** A/3 model.

< The **Iso Rivolta** of 1964 was a fast 2-plus-2 grand touring coupe from Bertone.

< In 1967 at the Frankfurt show, Bertone displayed a four door **Iso Rivolta,** the 'Fidia'.

Again the Corvette engine in a 2-plus-2 coupe body for **Iso Rivolta,** this time the 'Lele' of 1969. >

The style of Bertone, the parallel body lines highlighted at the rear of the 'Lele'.
ᐯ

The **Jaguar** XK150 in left-hand-drive form, with rather unsporting coachwork.

Those fins again! To many this Bertone **Jaguar** was not a success, most preferring the XK150 in its original form.

There is some doubt if this is another XK150 or Bertone's original creation tarted up with side air scoops.

Gandini illustration for the **Jaguar** FT. ⟩

First seen at Geneva in 1966 was this ⟩
**Jaguar** 420G with Bertone-designed
two door coachwork. Known as the
**Jaguar** FT, for Ferruccio Tarchini,
one gets the feeling that Bertone was
not relaxed with this British-built car.
∨

The front of the **Jaguar** 'Pirana' certainly resembles the Lamborghini Espada. The rear ... something for Citroen?

**Jaguar** fans had a shock at the 1967 London Motor show with this 'Pirana'.

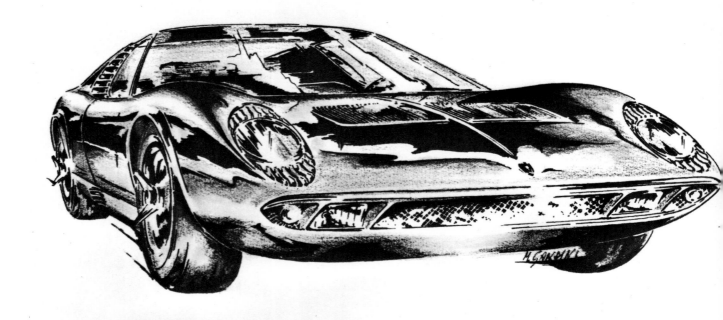

∧
Pencil sketch for the **Lamborghini** Miura from Gandini at Bertone.

Production Miura. Everything about ⟩ the car spelt speed and excitement.

Accessibility was the Miura's strong-⟩ point, but construction gave some headaches.

⟨One of Bertone's most famous creations for **Lamborghini,** the Miura. This is the prototype shown to the world in 1966.

500ª MIURA
BERTONE — LAMBORGHINI

Celebrations for the 500th completed **Lamborghini** Miura bodyshell.

For the 1968 Brussels motor show, Bertone had created the **Lamborghini** Miura roadster. The original coupe design lost none of its style when presented without a roof.

For **Lamborghini,** the Marzal in 1966. >

Not a practical design, many considered the Marzal too futuristic – including the boss of **Lamborghini!**
∨

Introduced by **Lamborghini** in 1967, this Italian car builder sold almost 1000 examples of Bertone's four-seater Espada.

The style of Bertone's Marzal can be clearly seen in the **Lamborghini** Espada; however making a production model from a prototype design invariably loses something.

The Japanese manufacturer **Mazda** went to Bertone in 1965 for a four-seater four door design on their popular 1500 chassis.

The production 1500 **Mazda** Luce with changed headlamps and a rather boxy saloon body to which, presumably, the Japanese motorist did not object.

1500CCの常識を破った6人乗り高速ツーリングサル

**MAZDA LUCE**

新発売

ルーチェは、1500ccクラス唯一の6人乗り、しかもOHC、78馬力、という、このクラス最高の性能を誇る、高速ツーリング設計の新しい

連続最高時速
ファミリーカーで

Naturally the Japanese manufacturer of a de Luxe model is obliged to offer its customers a Super de Luxe. Apart from the bonnet line the Bertone design for the Luce is unchanged. This is the 1800 **Mazda** chassis.

The coupe **Mazda** from Bertone was powered by the revolutionary rotary engine. The long sloping rear, without door pillar, lengthens the coupe body in an awkward fashion.

One has the impression that Bertone enjoyed this racing car design. The 1967 **Panther** powered by a formula one BRM engine. (175)

**The Panther** sports racing coupe remained a prototype; many likened it to the Chaparral 2F coupe from Jim Hall of Texas also in 1967. (176)

# The Seventies

Bertone designed an off-the-peg rally version of the Fiat 131 for **Abarth.** One can imagine the Italian street racers adapting to this little gem.

By 1975, Bertone had executed further design work on the **Abarth** which resulted in the 013. A rear wing was fitted and plenty of air scoops; the model was used successfully in the circuit of Italy rally.

An Alitalia-sponsored **Abarth** 131, a more civilised rally car with P7 Pirellis and no rear wing. The model is shown alongside a Stratos at Geneva in 1978.

Another dream car, inspired, like the 'Carabo', by the T33 Alfa Romeo. Shown by Bertone at Geneva in 1976, the **Alfa Romeo**-based 'Navajo'.

The heater/air controls, gear knob and bulkhead all used the cylindrical design; instrumentation was computerised, the steering wheel rational and the resulting interior functional and tidy.

Disappointing from the rear, the dream car was squared-off with a large double wing.

The bonnet retained the by now established style of **Citroen.** The car was created by Bertone as a one off in 1972 and titled 'Camargue'. Very short rear overhang, and kinked roof line, did not help a design which was rather uneasy.

For **Ferrari,** a targa-style creation on the 308GT chassis, rather appropriately called the 'Rainbow'. Shown in 1976, Bertone's Ferrari Rainbow displayed a most angular style not normally associated with Maranello products.

126

Introduced in 1972, the **Fiat** X1/9
from Bertone. The model was an im-
mediate success for the Fiat company,
and in 1974 voted 'Best styled car of
the year' by *Motor Trend* magazine.

**Fiat** X1/9 bodies leaving the Bertone
factory in 1974.

Illustrations showing the optional
equipment designed for the 'Village'.

Built in 1974, on **Fiat** 127 running
gear, the 'Village' was ideal for fun off-
road motoring.

Not unnaturally the popular **Fiat** X1/9 was a car which underwent many improvements and subtle design changes. This is the 'Corsa' of 1975.

The model was racing in Italy in 1976 in the Silhouette class. Thus a Bertone redesign of the X1/9 for competition use became necessary. The chassis and mechanics were assembled by Ing. Dallara, previously with Lamborghini. It can be imagined that this particular **Fiat** was extremely rapid.

Displayed at Geneva in 1977 a very special **Fiat** X1/9 originally intended exclusively for the Swiss market.

Owing to the sales success of the X1/9, **Fiat** tended to create luxurious versions of this model for sale in countries which the Fiat management considered as "unexplored markets".

In 1978 **Fiat** celebrated having sold 50,000 X1/9s by having Bertone build another special version. This special series had different instruments, spoiler, special paintwork and interior. >

The Italian 'Mini' by **Innocenti** and designed by Bertone. In the background can be seen the original shape that made the small car world-famous.

Bertone's design for **Innocenti** was crisp with no uneccessary frills.

The charming Ritmo ('Strada' in some markets) Cabrio S 85 for **Fiat,** displayed at Frankfurt in August 1979. In order to achieve the necessary body rigidity and strength Bertone completely redesigned the chassis structure.

The **Iso Rivolta** Grifo Can-Am of 1972. The engine was enlarged from 5733 to 7443cc using the Corvette engine. The design belied the car's speed and muscle.

The Bertone line accentuated on the 'Ascot' by the use of two-colour paintwork.

On the **Jaguar** XJS chassis the 'Ascot' in early 1977.

The interior of the **Jaguar** 'Ascot' was executed as one would expect of a luxury car, but the instrument binnacle was set high up and as a result received criticism. >

<An unusual mechanical specification from **Lamborghini** resulted in the Urraco. Bertone kept the overall height to a minimum yet still managed to incorporate a rear seat in this transverse V8 engine car.

<The rear end treatment of the **Lamborghini** Urraco had a relaxed and pleasing style.

The prototype for the incredible **Lamborghini** Countach from Bertone in 1973.
∨

Coded 'LP 400' the **Lamborghini** Countach was a true supercar.

The 'Bravo', first seen in 1974, remained a prototype.

The 'Bravo' had that unmistakable Bertone style from the rear ... even the rear glass treatment.

Using the same mechanicals as the Urraco, the three-litre **Lamborghini** 'Bravo' with Bertone's wedge design.

The **Lancia** Stratos in refined prototype form, clearly illustrating compact style and beautiful lines.

A prototype for the **Lancia** 'Stratos' by Bertone. Seen at Turin in 1970 this design was built on the Lancia 1600HF chassis. Bertone could have used the frontal design for his Countach.

The fabulous **Lancia** Stratos which Bertone created in 1972.

A Stratos body passing through the Bertone factory in 1974.

**Lancia** Stratos 'Silhouette' of 1976. >

Stratos production car of 1974; the coachbuilder's motif has quite rightly been enlarged.

143

< Rally version of the Stratos seen at Geneva in 1977.

The rally Stratos of 1978. Its extra equipment and sponsorship decals could not disguise the unique creation from Bertone.
∨

Wooden model of the **Lancia** 'Sibilo'. >

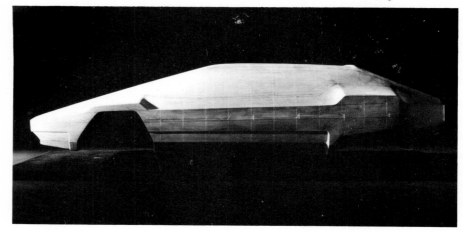

A Bertone creation continuing the >
Stratos theme for **Lancia.** The 'Sibilo' >
of 1978. Bertone in endeavouring to
reduce the overall height, 'drops' the
coachwork down between the wheel
arches. The rear is awkward; the
wheelarch design fresh.

Interior of the 'Sibilo', which was
steered by a giant 'button'.
∨

For **Maserati** Bertone created the 'Khamsin' of 1973. A truly gorgeous-looking Grand Touring car.

The Citroen-influenced **Maserati** series II Quattroporte as seen in 1974 powered by the V6 engine. Bertone created a deep rake for the windscreen which gave a pleasantly false impression of overall size, for it was a large motor car.

Built upon the mechanics of an **NSU** RO80 Bertone introduced the 'Trapeze' in 1973. Incredibly it was a four-seater! The mid-engine was located lengthways, so that the rear passengers could sit each side of it; an ingenious ergonomic solution, but practical?

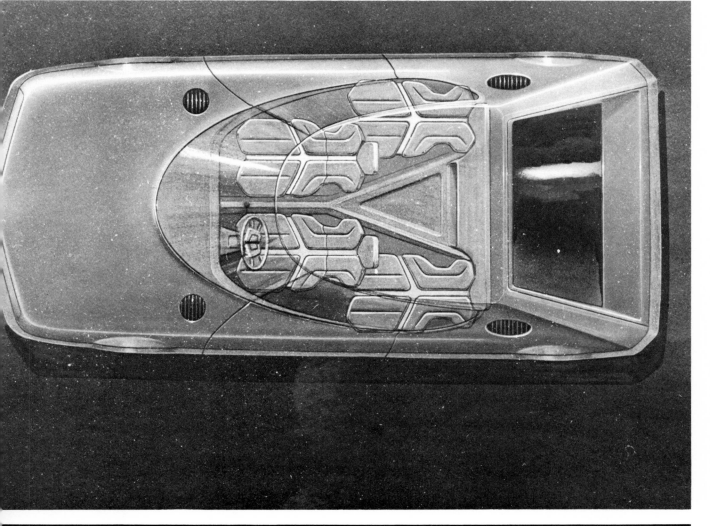

Not to be left out of the American dune-buggy fashion, Bertone's 1970 'Shake'. Based on the **Simca** 1200S, in the final analysis one dune buggy looks much like another.

A sort of pick-up cum dune buggy, this design was based on a tiny **Suzuki** chassis.

The luxuriously equipped **Volvo** 264TE of 1976. Aimed at defence of the Swedish luxury car market from Mercedes-Benz and Rolls-Royce.

Sporting luxury in **Volvo's** 262C, Bertone building this version in 1977. There were few complaints about interior quality, layout or workmanship! (227 & 228)

Based upon production **Volvo** 343 running gear, Bertone designed the 'Tundra' in 1979. The famous grille and badge has not been lost. (229)

  # The Eighties

Interior of the two-seater **Alfa Romeo** Delfino, clean design and loaded with electronic gadgets. Outside, generous glass area, large luggage compartment and a careful aerodynamic shape blending glass and steel in true Bertone style. (229C & 229D)

Shown in March 1983 at the Geneva International Motor Show, Bertone's interpretation of an **Alfa Romeo** coupe. Constructed on the Alfa 6 chassis and running gear, but with increased front and rear track, Bertone's 'Delfino' is aimed at the market for larger GT cars. (229A &

An important experience for Bertone early in 1982. The X1/9 was now to be marketed directly by his company under a new Fiat-Bertone agreement.

The delightful cabriolet Ritmo (Strada in some markets) Super 85 exhibited at Geneva in 1982.

Bertone neatly redesigned the rear end so that hood storage and carrying capacity were not problems.

Seen at the Frankfurt Motor Show in August 1983, the Cabrio marketed by Bertone. Four years after its introduction the model has matured and sales continue to be high.

This spectacular Bertone Cabrio has interior upholstered in leather and mink fur by Gianfranco Togno, one of Italy's best known furriers. The amiable cuddly toy was not an optional extra!

Style it certainly has. Should this **Lamborghini** ever be a production model it will be interesting to see what transpires with the rear design ...

A different sort of roadster for **Lamborghini** in 1980, the 'Athon'.

Bertone has the last word on steering wheel design. The television screen takes the place of instruments and the steering is by means of a moving track which rotates in almost rectangular orbit. Bertone called this an "ultra simple dashboard". (236)

Seen at Turin in April 1982 the **Mazda** MX-81. (235)

# The Other Bertone Designs

Before the war commercial bodies were big and necessary business for Bertone. Here an ambulance body on a **Lancia** Artena chassis.

A privately-operated motor coach, based on a **Lancia** chassis, with rear entrance for fourteen passengers.

A **Lancia** long-distance trucking outfit complete with boxed drawbar trailer, which must have been fun over the Alps!

∧ A Bertone constructed milk lorry on a **Lancia** chassis. (240)

‹ Another passenger vehicle, this time with very square coachwork and curtains. (241)

A familiar name and a lovely little pre-› war **Fiat** commercial. (242)

≪ Stratos helmet from Bertone in 1973.

‹ A scooter for **Innocenti** in 1967, the Lui.

On the quayside a Bertone design, the ›
**Lamborghini** Espada; on the water his
design for a fast luxury motor boat the
**Crestliner** Clipper 37 in 1970.

‹ For the French commercial vehicle
manufacturer **Saviem,** two Bertone designs for middle-weight commercial
vehicles in 1975.

A nautical appearance remained in the ›
Clipper, although Bertone's wheel and
instrument cowls were a fresh
approach for this industry.

# Index

| | |
|---|---|
| A.S.A. | 86. |
| Abarth | 30, 31, 32, 33, 76, 122. |
| Alfa Romeo | 34, 35, 39, 40, 41, 42, 43, 44, 77, 78, 79, 80, 81, 82, 83. |
| Arnott | 45, 46, 47, 48, 49, 50, 51, 52, 53. |
| Aston Martin | 87. |
| Autobianchi | 88, 89. |
| | |
| B.A.T. | 35, 36, 37, 38. |
| BMW | 92, 93, 94. |
| Bentley | 54. |
| Bizzarini | 90, 91. |
| Borgward | 54. |
| | |
| Ceirano | 14. |
| Chevrolet | 97. |
| Citroen | 124. |
| | |
| Diatto | 14. |
| Dodge | 55. |
| | |
| Ferrari | 55, 95, 96, 125. |
| Fiat | 15, 16, 17, 18, 19, 20, 21, 22, 23, 56, 57, 58, 59, 60, 61, 98, 99, 100, 101, 126, 127, 128, 129, 130, 131, 133, 154, 155, 163. |
| Ford | 102. |
| | |
| Gordon Keeble | 103. |
| | |
| Healey | 62. |
| | |
| Innocenti | 132, 164. |
| ISO | 91, 104, 105, 106, 107, 133 |
| | |
| Jaguar | 108, 109, 110, 111, 134, 135. |
| | |
| Lamborghini | 112, 113, 114, 115, 116, 117, 136, 137, 138, 139, 156, 157, 165. |
| Lancia | 23, 24, 25, 26, 27, 62, 63, 140, 141, 142, 143, 144, 145, 160, 161, 162. |
| | |
| Maserati | 64, 146. |
| Mazda | 118, 119, 158. |
| | |
| N.S.U. | 65, 147. |
| | |
| O.S.C.A. | 66, 67. |
| | |
| Panther | 120, 121. |
| | |
| S.P.A. | 28. |
| Saviem | 164. |
| Siata | 68, 69. |
| Simca | 70, 71, 148. |
| Stanguellini | 72, 73, 74. |
| Suzuki | 149. |
| | |
| Volvo | 149, 150. |

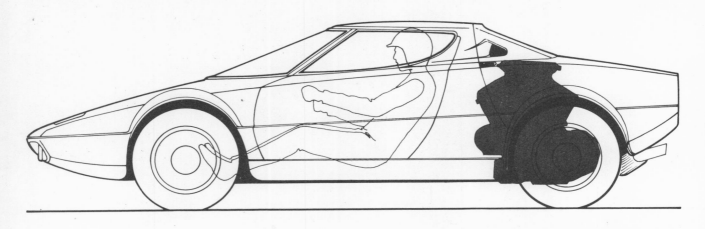

1971 - Lancia STRATOS HF

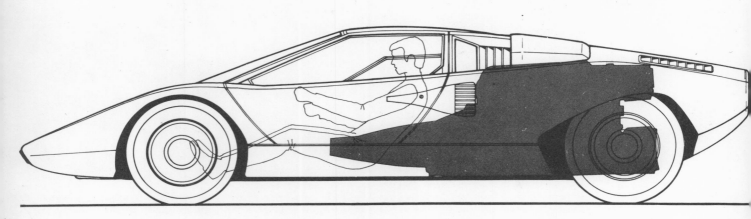

1971 - Lamborghini COUNTACH

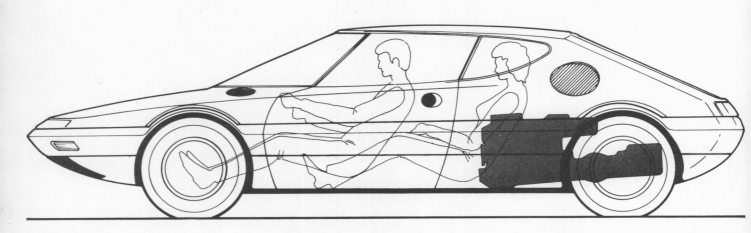

1973 - Audi NSU TRAPEZE